Volmir Sergio Marchioro

Association of molecular markers with panicle weight in oats

Volmir Sergio Marchioro

Association of molecular markers with panicle weight in oats

Using different plant management methods as a selection strategy

ScienciaScripts

Imprint
Any brand names and product names mentioned in this book are subject to trademark, brand or patent protection and are trademarks or registered trademarks of their respective holders. The use of brand names, product names, common names, trade names, product descriptions etc. even without a particular marking in this work is in no way to be construed to mean that such names may be regarded as unrestricted in respect of trademark and brand protection legislation and could thus be used by anyone.

Cover image: www.ingimage.com

This book is a translation from the original published under ISBN 978-3-330-75977-0.

Publisher:
Sciencia Scripts
is a trademark of
Dodo Books Indian Ocean Ltd. and OmniScriptum S.R.L publishing group

120 High Road, East Finchley, London, N2 9ED, United Kingdom
Str. Armeneasca 28/1, office 1, Chisinau MD-2012, Republic of Moldova, Europe
Printed at: see last page
ISBN: 978-620-8-31101-8

CONTENTS

1 INTRODUCTION

Plant breeding programs are constantly developing new selection techniques with the aim of improving those conventionally used, thus the recent interest in technological advances such as molecular markers. Through this technique it is possible to reliably access an individual's genotype rather than just its phenotype, thus being able to assess the genetic variability that exists within and between different species and use it in genetic improvement programs.

The development of molecular techniques for genetic analysis has increased the amount of information available for understanding the genetic structure of cereals. With the use of these techniques, it is possible to identify and transfer desirable genes between improved varieties, as well as the introgression of genes from wild species. Polygenic traits, commonly referred to as quantitative traits, which are difficult to analyze using traditional methodologies, are being easily improved and understood using molecular marker techniques.

Therefore, with the use of these techniques, together with knowledge of quantitative genetics and segregating populations, it is possible to select new genetic constitutions with great certainty. As a result, the selection of superior genitors in breeding programs can be carried out objectively and precisely, determining the formation of segregating populations with a high frequency of superior individuals.

The different types of molecular markers available today differ in the technique used to reveal variability at the deoxyribonucleic acid (DNA) level. The *Amplified Fragment Length Polymorphisms* (AFLP) molecular marker technique is being widely used, combining the specificity of *Restriction Fragment Length Polymorphism* (RFLP) *restriction* sites with the practicality of *Polymerase chain reaction* (PCR) amplification, making it a powerful tool for genome characterization and genetic mapping (Vos et al., 1995). One of the advantages of AFLP is its great power to detect genetic variability, since the technique exploits restriction and amplification polymorphisms. AFLP combines the advantage of exploring arbitrary genomic regions, without the need for prior knowledge of DNA sequences, with the high specificity of the PCR technique. Associated with this, analysis by segregant blocks using the *Bulk Segregant Analysis* (BSA) technique, proposed by Michelmore et al. (1991), can be useful, especially for identifying regions of the genome that have not yet been covered.

Most economically important traits are under complex genetic control, involving the action of several genes, which makes them difficult to manipulate and understand. Genomic regions containing gene loci associated with such quantitative traits are called Quantitative Trait Loci (QTL). The ability to detect QTL using molecular markers is a function of the magnitude of the effect of the QTL and the size of the population under study.

The aim of this study was to verify the association of molecular markers with the genomic region(s) responsible for the expression of the panicle weight trait in oats, using the AFLP molecular analysis technique.

2. LITERATURE review

2.1. Growing oats

Due to its various uses, oats are an economically viable alternative for cultivation during the cold season in the southern region of Brazil. The inclusion of this crop in production systems leads to improvements in the physical, chemical and biological properties of the soil, the reduction of diseases and pests of other crops and the allelopathic control of weeds. It also makes it possible to produce grain used in human and animal food, to form pastures, to make hay and to use as a green or dead cover for the soil.

2.1.1. Origin and domestication of oats

The origin of cultivated oats, like all cereals, was lost in ancient times. Wheat and barley were initially more important than oats to man and there is evidence that this cereal persisted as an invasive plant in crops for centuries before being cultivated (Coffman, 1961).

As these crops were dispersed to the cold environments of central and northern Europe, oats became more competitive and were finally domesticated as an alternative crop. The determining factors in the domestication of oats are not known, but it seems that greater adaptation to cold climates was fundamental. Introduced to Brazil by European discoverers and immigrants, it was only in the 1990s that it became a crop of economic importance (Tavares et al., 1993).

2.1.2. Botanical description of oats

Oats belong to the family Poaceae, subfamily Poideae, tribe Aveneae and genus *Avena*. The species of the *Avena* genus occur at three d2.e ploidy levels: diploids 2n=2x=14, tetraploids 2n=4x=28 and hexaploids 2n=6x=42, (Tavares et al., 1993). The main oat species and their respective ploidy levels are included in Table 1 (Federizzi et al. 1999).

Table 1 - Main oat species and their ploidy levels.

Species	Ploidy level	Species	Ploidy level
Avena strigosa	2n=2x=14	*Avena hirtula*	2n=2x=14
Avena atlantica	2n=2x=14	*Avena wiestii*	2n=2x=14
Avena canariensis	2n=2x=14	*Avena damascena*	2n=2x=14
Avena prostrata	2n=2x=14	*Avena longiglumis*	2n=2x=14
Avena clauda	2n=2x=14	*Avena ventricosa*	2n=2x=14
Avena barbata	2n=4x=28	*Avena abyssinica*	2n=4x=28
Avena vaviloviana	2n=4x=28	*Avena marrocana*	2n=4x=28
Avena murphy	2n=4x=28	*Avena macrostachya*	2n=4x=28
Avena sterilis	2n=6x=42	*Avena fàtua*	2n=6x=42
Avena sativa	2n=6x=42	*Avena nuda*	2n=6x=42

2.1.3. Improving oats

Plant breeding consists of creating variability, selecting desirable genotypes and testing them in different environments for an adjustment that will allow the maximum expression of their potential, thus being able to identify superior genotypes and, necessarily, the existence of variability in the constitution of the population. According to Tavares et al. (1993), the absence of variability to any degree will render the most intense of selection actions ineffective.

Improvement of the oat crop has gone through different periods in southern Brazil, starting with the development of cultivars with a long cycle, high stature and low yield; then the introduction of strains through exchanges with international institutions, with better grain quality, lower plant stature and average grain yield; finally, the development of genotypes by local institutions, mainly the Federal University of Rio Grande do Sul (UFRGS) and the University of Passo Fundo (UPF), with new plant architecture, greater precocity, better grain quality and, above all, high grain yield potential (Carvalho & Federizzi, 1989). According to Federizzi et al. (1998), the result of this stage in the improvement of oats was the emergence of small-scale industries for the processing and transformation of grain into healthier products for the human diet.

The great challenge for oat breeders is to make genotypes with high industrial quality permanently available and also to identify genetic constitutions that surpass the grain yield expressed by the cultivars on the market (Brown & Forsberg, 1987). However, in view of the increase in the area cultivated with oats, it is essential that breeding is dynamic, fast and economically efficient. However, in order to achieve this goal, McGinnis & Shebeski (1968) have reported on the importance of a selection method capable of guaranteeing the choice of the best genotypes, especially in terms of quantitative traits, in highly segregating populations.

2.1.4. Selection environment

The existence of differentiated responses of genotypes to the effects of the environment has often been observed in various species of cultivated plants. As well as influencing genetic gains, this interaction makes it difficult to recommend genotypes for different environments.

Interaction causes difficulties in breeding, as it indicates the inconsistency of the genotype's superiority in relation to the variance of the environment, i.e. there are genotypes with better performance in one environment, but not in others, making selection and recommendation more difficult (Cruz & Castoldi, 1991). In this way, identifying the best environment for increasing the efficiency of the breeding program, especially in terms of grain yield, has been another major obstacle for breeders (Hill et al., 1998), basically because of the costs associated with this process (Allen et al., 1977) and the need to identify genetic constitutions with adaptability to all the areas where oats are grown in southern Brazil.

According to Atlin & Frey (1990), few studies have been carried out in an attempt to overcome this difficulty. Byrne et al. (1995) suggest three selection strategies: a) carried out in environments that promote the maximization of variation and genetic gain, based on the increase in heritability; b) tested in environments (Blum, 1998) as representative as possible of the area of the crop to be improved; and c) using environments in these two conditions, alternately, to identify genetic constitutions adjusted to both situations (Calhoun et al., 1994). According to Ceccarelli et al. (1998), many breeders in developed countries adopt the first strategy, because the presence of high productivity environments determines greater efficiency in the manifestation of environmental variance, improving the expression of genetic differences and also increasing heritability compared to low productivity environments. Ceccarelli (1989) stated that the high genetic potential of genotypes is only maintained up to a limit of environmental stress and, within this range, the heritability estimate can often be high. According to Falconer (1981), grain yield in low and high productivity environments can be considered as distinct characteristics, not necessarily determined by the effects of the same alleles that govern their expression.

2.1.5. Selection in segregating generations

Various studies have demonstrated the need to create new criteria to modify the techniques conventionally used in the improvement of cool-season cereals (Santos & Carvalho, 1977; Cruz et al., 1983), and to establish criteria for recognizing genetic differences and environmental effects with greater accuracy.

When selection is carried out in highly segregating generations, based on the individual plant, the effects of non-additive gene action (dominance and epistasis) contribute to deviations in the expected phenotypic value and also make it difficult to choose a superior individual due to the participation of heterosis (Seitzer & Evans, 1978). According to Carvalho (1982), another difficulty with this selection mechanism is the substitution of a large number of alleles at different loci to determine progress in the trait. Fasoulas (1973), working with plant selection using the genealogical method, did not obtain efficiency in selecting for high grain yields in the F2 generation, due to the lack of correlation between the selected plants and the F3 progeny tested. McGinnis & Shebeski (1968) obtained similar results, where the progenies of selected plants and plants taken at random in F2 generations did not differ in grain yield. According to Sampson (1971), the genealogical method is the least appropriate for selection in generations with intense segregation, and the use of the mass method, with plants in competition, can lead to much more promising results, since in unstable environments natural selection is very important and seems to be more efficient.

Studying the effect of different selection methods in wheat on highly segregating populations, Cruz et al. (1983) found that for many characters, including grain yield, there was high evidence that individual plant selection, based on quantitative measurements, with subsequent pooling of superior individuals (*bulk*), contributed directly to the genetic progress of the selected population. This aspect could be the main reason for the better performance of the hive and mass selection mechanisms on the SSD (*Single Seed Descendant*), under the conditions tested and for this objective. Mass selection is an old but often efficient selection method for improving oats (Geadelmann & Frey, 1975), especially when there is intense competition. According to Chandhanamutta & Frey (1973), the use of this method through grain yield components revealed increases of 5.6% in grain yield. According to Knott (1972), one of the alternatives for increasing the efficiency of selection for grain yield in highly segregating generations would be to reduce the effects of the environment, increasing heritability and, consequently, the efficiency of selection. In view of this fact, Allard (1999) considered that the breeder is almost always led to use a very subjective judgment system, based only on quick visual selections, instead of more precise evaluations. More recently, Quail et al. (1989) reported that selection in highly segregating generations, aimed at a particular type of plant, is applied at different levels of intensity and, even with the possibility of selecting for characters linked to grain yield, can be considered subjective. Under these conditions, they state that even in genotypes that are well adjusted to the environment, it is difficult to identify high yield potential in generations of intense segregation. According to Cruz et al. (1983), selection on quantitative traits in unstable environments merits further study, especially in the development of mechanisms that make it possible to identify a greater correlation between the genotype and phenotype of superior individuals.

2.1.6. The use of panicle weight in indirect selection

Panicle weight in oats includes the combination of two of the three components of grain yield: grains per panicle and grain weight. Research into estimating the heritability of these components has resulted in a wide range of coefficients and has contributed to a better understanding of the correlation between these components and grain yield. Many researchers have reported medium to high heritability coefficients for spikelets per panicle, and a positive correlation with grain yield. Similarly, high heritability and a positive correlation with yield have been found for grain weight (Chapko & Brinkman, 1991). According to Chandhanamutta & Frey (1973), 80% of the increase in grain yield in oats can be attributed to the increase in the number of grains per panicle, and 20% to the increase in grain weight. Due to this contribution of the components of grain yield, Brown & Forsberg (1987) pointed to evidence of a positive relationship between panicle weight and grain yield (Chapko & Brinkman, 1991), justifying the application of indirect selection through this character.

Chapko & Brinkman (1991), evaluating the relationship between panicle weight, grain yield and its components in oats, found a high positive correlation between panicle weight and grain yield (0.54 - 0.84).

According to Sampson (1971), panicle weight in oats has great potential for the indirect selection of superior lines in segregating generations; however, he specifies that for success to be achieved, selection must be carried out in the field and on plants with reduced spacing (high competitiveness). Under these conditions, other studies have also shown the effectiveness of increasing grain yield in segregating generations through indirect selection of yield components, such as McNeal et al. (1978) in wheat, Valentine (1983) in barley and Gravois & McNew (1993) in rice.

2.2. Genetic dissimilarity in plant breeding

Knowledge of differences in genetic constitutions has been of great importance for any breeding program. This importance is related to the need to identify genitors with genetic differences that can produce progenies with greater heterosis, thus increasing the probability of obtaining superior individuals (Cruz & Regazzi, 1997).

Measures of genetic dissimilarity, as a way of characterizing and identifying distinct genetic constituencies of different species, determined by reproductive isolation, have aroused the interest of several authors (Santos et al. 1997; Gaur *et al.* 1978; Casler, 1995). Among the measures of dissimilarity, which can show the intensity of genetic variability, the Euclidean and Mahalanobis distances are the most commonly used by breeders in plant breeding programs. According to Gaur et al. (1978), multivariate analysis can be used as a powerful tool to estimate genetic dissimilarity in order to help choose genetic constituents that may result, through their progenies, in superior combinations. According to Machado (1999), this technique is the most efficient and widely used for identifying genetic dissimilarity.

Another important technique in the study of genetic dissimilarity is cluster analysis, which, according to Cruz & Regazzi (1997), aims to gather and classify genotypes into various groups in such a way that there is homogeneity within and heterogeneity between the groups formed. The most commonly used clustering methods in plant breeding programs have been hierarchical and optimization methods. In hierarchical methods, the genitors are grouped by a process that is repeated at various levels until a dendogram is established.

In optimization methods, the set of genitors is partitioned into mutually exclusive subgroups by maximizing or minimizing a pre-established measure (Cruz & Regazzi, 1997).

The degree of genetic dissimilarity between genotypes can be estimated using the Mahalanobis statistic ($D2$) based on the means of the genotypes and the residual covariance matrix. To group the genotypes, the hierarchical nearest neighbor method can be used to form dendograms, which consists of identifying the most similar genotypes in the dissimilarity matrix, forming an initial group and, from this group, estimating the distances from the other genotypes.

In the study of genetic dissimilarity between genotypes, it is possible to estimate the relative importance of each character evaluated in terms of the genetic dissimilarity observed between genotypes, This is done by analyzing the coefficients of the linear transformations to obtain the canonical variables, according to Cruz (1990), and by dividing the components D^2 , relative to each trait, into the total genetic dissimilarity observed, according to Singh's recommendation (1981).

2.3. Molecular markers in plant breeding

Increasing the efficiency of selection, better knowledge and characterization of germplasm and maximizing genetic gains have been the goals of plant breeders all over the world. New ways of achieving these goals have been constantly pursued by plant breeding. Hence the interest in technologies such as molecular markers. These offer breeders the possibility of accessing an individual's genotype rather than just its phenotype. Because the phenotype is the expression of the genotype under specific environmental conditions, it can change under different conditions due to non-genetic factors. However, the genotype, or DNA makeup of an individual, remains the same throughout its life cycle. Selecting the phenotype is like chasing a moving target that changes with the environment. Selecting on the basis of an individual's genotype can avoid this problem, although it may seem difficult. New molecular marker techniques make it possible to access and select traits at the DNA level.

Molecular markers are DNA characteristics that differentiate two or more individuals and are genetically inherited. The different types of molecular markers available today can be differentiated by the technique used to reveal variability at the DNA level. Various molecular marker techniques such as RFLP *(Restriction Fragments Length Polymorphism*) (Botstein et al., 1980), RAPD *(Random Amplified Polymorphism DNA)* (Williams et al., 1990), AFLP *(Amplified Fragments Length Polymorphism*) (Vos *et al.,* 1995), SSR *(Simple Sequence Repeats*) (Morgante and Olivieri 1993) and ISSR *(Inter-Simple Sequence Repeats*) (Bornet & Branchard, 2001) have been developed and are being widely used as auxiliary tools in breeding programs. Mainly because they access the entire genome of the organism and, more importantly, are not influenced by the environment.

The available literature on the application of AFLP molecular markers in plant breeding is very abundant, ranging from their use in simple genetic dissimilarity studies in wheat (Barrett & Kidwell 1998; Barrett et al. 1998; Burkhamer et al. 1998), barley (*Hordeum vulgare* L.) (Ellis et al. 1997; Schut et al. 1997), maize (*Zea mays* L.) (Ajmone Marsan et al. 1998), lettuce (*Lactuca* sp. L.) (Hill et al. 1996), sunflower (*Helianthus annuus* L.) (Hongtrakul et al. 1997) and soybean (*Glycine max* L.) (VanToai et al. 1997). AFLP has also been used to build high-density genetic maps in Barley (*Hordeum vulgare* L.) (Becker et al. 1995; Qi & Lindhout 1997), Rice (*Oryza sativa* L.) (Maheswaran et al. 1997), Soybean (*G. max* L.) (Keim *et al.* 1997), Melon (*Cucumis melo* L.) (Wang et al. 1997) and in the analysis of quantitative traits (QTLs) (Pakniyat et al. 1997; Powell et al. 1997; Roa et al. 1997).

The *Bulk Segregant Analysis* (BSA) methodology, proposed by Michelmore et al. (1991), has contributed greatly to the study of segregating populations. The BSA methodology maximizes the choice of genomic regions associated with a given trait as long as it combines several genetic constitutions. In order to identify a marker that confers polymorphism to two or more contrasting *bulks*, it is necessary to extract DNA from *bulks*, preferably from advanced generations, that are contrasting for a given trait. In this way, plants are grouped into two phenotypic classes (*bulks)* by mixing plant material, or DNA already extracted, from at least ten plants with the same phenotype. This way we can be sure that in most of the genotypes that make up the *bulk* there is a common sequence, which belongs to the sequence of the gene that codes for the trait. In this way, the *bulks* are only genotypically different with regard to the analyzed trait. Using any molecular marker technique, in this case AFLP, it is possible to find *primers* capable of amplifying the DNA of one *bulk* and not that of the other.

When all (or the majority) of the *bulks* that are phenotypically the same with regard to the trait under study show the band and all (or the minority) of the *bulks* lacking the trait under study do not show the band, it can be inferred that the amplified segment is linked or partially linked to the gene of interest. For its part, the AFLP technique (Vos et al., 1995) stands out for the abundant polymorphism it detects at the level of the entire genome. Thus, the combination of a marker technique with a good capacity for detecting polymorphism, as in the case of AFLP, combined with the analysis of segregating blocks, which maximizes the identification of genomic regions associated with a given trait, can be very useful, especially for identifying regions of the genome associated with quantitative trait loci (QTL).

2.3.1. AFLP molecular markers

The AFLP technique has been and is being widely used, combining the specificity of the RFLP restriction sites with the practicality of PCR amplification, suggesting it as a powerful tool in genome characterization and genetic mapping (Vos *et al.*, 1995). The technique is based on the simultaneous digestion of genomic DNA with two restriction enzymes. Specific adapters, with ends complementary to the cohesive ends of the restriction sites, are attached to the digested DNA fragments. Two specific adapters are used, one for each restriction site.

The digested fragments with the adapters attached to them are subjected to a PCR reaction with pre-selective *primers*, whose sequence is complementary to that of the adapters, plus an arbitrary nucleotide at their 3' end. Pre-selective amplification is carried out in order to increase the proportion of fragments of interest with restriction sites and to make an initial selection of these fragments. The pre-amplified fragments are submitted to selective amplification reactions, using *primers* with the same sequence as the pre-selective *primers* plus two arbitrary nucleotides at their 3' end. The polymorphic fragments are detected on sequencing gels.

One of the advantages of AFLP is its great power to detect genetic variability, since the technique exploits restriction and amplification polymorphisms. In this way, a large number of polymorphic fragments can be resolved in a single sequencing gel. As the *primers* used in the amplification stages are long, around 20 base pairs, the specificity of the reactions is significantly increased when compared to RAPD. Thus, AFLP combines the advantage of exploring arbitrary genomic regions, without the need for prior knowledge of DNA sequences, with the high specificity of the PCR technique.

2.3.2. Molecular markers and complex characters

Most of the characters of economic importance, both for plants and animals, are quantitative in nature, i.e. they are metric characters with a continuous distribution. Therefore, the distinction between genes related to Mendelian traits and those related to quantitative traits lies in the magnitude of their effects. When a given trait is governed by one or a few genes, each of which has a large effect on the trait and is little influenced by environmental effects, segregation will be discontinuous (Mendelian segregation), forming a few phenotypic classes that are easily distinguishable from one another. On the other hand, another trait which is governed by several genes (*polygenes)*, each gene having a small effect and highly influenced by the effects of the environment, segregation will be continuous (simultaneous segregation of several genes), forming a large number of phenotypic classes, increasing the difficulty of distinguishing between classes. Genomic regions containing gene loci associated with such quantitative traits are called QTLs. The ability to detect QTLs using molecular markers is a function of the magnitude of the QTL effect and the size of the population under study.

3. DEVELOPMENT OF THE STUDY

The work was carried out in three different stages, seeking a better understanding of the methods used to breed segregating oat populations and their effects on genetic similarity and the identification of genes linked to the panicle weight trait.

3.1. First stage of the study: material and methods

The experiment was set up in the experimental field of the Genomics and Plant Breeding Center (CGF) of the Eliseu Maciel Agronomy Faculty (FAEM) - UFPel, in the municipality of Capâo do Leâo, in the 2000 agricultural year. Eight segregating oat populations in the F3 generation were included in the experiment. These populations were sown using three different sowing methods: spaced plant, full row and pit, the latter described as the *Hill* method by Frey (1965), which consists of sowing in pits, with a set number of seeds per pit. The design used in the experiment was randomized complete blocks, with two replications. In the pit sowing method, the plots were made up of ten pits with 15 seeds per pit, spaced 45 cm apart. In the spaced plant sowing method, the plots were made up of ten 2 m long rows spaced 20 cm apart between rows and between plants and in the full row sowing method, the plots were made up of two 2 m long rows with 60 suitable seeds per linear meter.

After ripening, all the panicles in the three sowing methods of the eight segregating populations were harvested, selecting for this study only the UFRGS 14 x OR 2 population from contrasting genitors for panicle weight, UFRGS 14 and OR 2 having high and low panicle weight, respectively. The panicles in this population were weighed and those weighing more than the average plus one standard deviation, as well as those weighing less than the average minus one standard deviation, within each pit, within each row of spaced plants and within each full row were selected.

Once the selected panicles had been threshed, the grains were grouped in *bulk*, forming pairs with the heaviest panicles and another with the least heavy within each pit, within each spaced plant row and within each full row, as shown in Table 2.

In 2001, the seeds from each of the 46 treatments (44 *bulks* plus the genitors) were sown in three plastic cups with ten seeds per cup. When the second leaf had formed, a small leaf sample was taken from six plants in each of the three cups of each treatment. These small samples were grouped together to form a larger sample of 18 plants. At the Laboratory of the Center for Genomics and Plant Breeding of the Eliseu Maciel School of Agronomy - UFPel, these samples were subjected to DNA extraction using the method described by Doyle & Doyle (1987).

The AFLP molecular analysis technique was used for the molecular study, following the protocol developed by Life Technologies, Inc - GIBCO. After *screening* to select *primer* pairs capable of generating polymorphisms between the genitors (UFRGS 14 and OR 2), the *primer* pairs listed in Table 3 were selected for the study.

Table 2 - Ratio of *bulks* formed with selection for panicle weight in the UFRGS 14 x OR 2 population in the three sowing methods plus the genitors.

Treatment	Immediately
1 Sel. cova - upper	24 Sel. spaced plant - bottom
2 Sel. pit - bottom	25 Sel. spaced plant - top
3 Sel. cova - upper	26 Sel. spaced plant - bottom
4 Pit seal - bottom	27 Sel. spaced plant - top
5 Sel. cova - upper	28 Sel. spaced plant - bottom
6 Pit seal - bottom	29 Spaced plant seal - top
7 Sel. cova - upper	30 Sel. spaced plant - bottom
8 Pit seal - bottom	31 Spaced plant seal - top

9 Sel. cova - upper

10 Pit seal - bottom

11 Sel. cova - upper

12 Pit seal - bottom

13 Sel. cova - superior

14 Pit seal - bottom

15 Sel. cova - upper

16 Pit seal - bottom

17 Sel. cova - superior

18 Pit seal - bottom

19 Sel. cova - superior

20 Pit seal - bottom

21 Sel. spaced plant - top

22 Sel. spaced plant - bottom

23 Spaced plant seal - top

32 Spaced plant seal - bottom

33 Spaced plant seal - top

34 Sel. spaced plant - bottom

35 Sel. spaced plant - top

36 Sel. spaced plant - bottom

37 Spaced plant seal - top

38 Spaced plant seal - bottom

39 Spaced plant seal - top

40 Sel. spaced plant - bottom

41 Full line seal - top

42 Full line seal - bottom

43 Full line seal - top

44 Full line seal - bottom

45 Genitor - UFRGS 14

46 Parent - OR 2

Table 3 - AFLP *primers* used in the study of populations subjected to three different breeding methods during the selection process.

Cutting of the MseI restriction enzyme		Cutting the restriction enzyme EcoRI	
Primer	Selective bases	*Primer*	Selective bases
M	CAA	E	AAC
M	CTA	E	AAG
M	CTG	E	ACC
M	CTC	E	ACT
M	CAC	E	ACA

To the amplification product was added 2/3 of its volume of loading buffer (98% formamide, 10 mM EDTA pH 8.0, 0.025% bromophenol blue and 0.025% xylene cyanol), followed by denaturation at 94°C for 6 minutes and application to a 6% acrylamide gel under denaturing conditions. The electrophoretic run was carried out in a *HOEFER SQ3 Sequencer* manual sequencing vat for approximately 2 hours at a constant power of 60 watts. The amplified fragments were revealed according to the silver nitrate staining protocol (Briard et al, 2000).

The bands were analyzed based on the electrophoretic pattern of the parents. In this way, all the polymorphic bands between the parents were evaluated in the segregating *bulks*.

The results obtained were submitted to the construction of a dissimilarity matrix between the treatments evaluated in this study, based on the calculation of the Jaccard similarity coefficient (Dias, 1998), coding the presence of the band on the gel as "1" and its absence as "0". The Jaccard coefficient between pairs of genotypes is given by $s_{ij} = a/a + b + c$, where "a" is the number of loci common to genotypes *i* and *j,* while "b" and "c" are the numbers of loci present only in each of the genotypes. From the dissimilarity matrix, the dendogram was obtained using the nearest neighbor technique, which consists of identifying the most similar genotypes in the dissimilarity matrix, forming an initial group and, from this group, the distances from the other genotypes were estimated. These analyses were carried out using the computer program Genes, developed by Cruz, 2001.

3.2. First stage of the study: results and discussion

In the study of the UFRGS 14 x OR 2 population, a total of 99 bands were obtained for the five pairs of *primers* tested. The highest number of bands found in a single analysis was for the M- CAA/E-AAC *primer* pair, with 24 bands, and the lowest number for the M- CTC/E-ACT *primer* pair, with only 14 bands. *Primer* pairs M-CTA/E-AAG, M-CTG/E-ACC and M-CAC/E-ACA revealed 21,

20 and 20 bands, respectively. The percentage of polymorphic bands between the *bulks* from the selection for high panicle weight and low panicle weight, in the three sowing methods in pit, spaced plant and full row was 9% on average. The same percentage of polymorphic bands (9%) was found between the genitors of the population under study, UFRGS 14 and OR 2.

Figure 1 shows the frequency of polymorphic bands between the *bulks* formed with the selection of heavier panicles against the selection of lighter panicles, in the three sowing methods. For the five pairs of *primers* tested, a higher frequency of polymorphic bands was observed among the *bulks* from the selection in the pit sowing method, when compared to the spaced plant and full row sowing methods. This fact is evidence of the hypothesis that the environment's participation in the expression of the phenotype during the selection process probably occurred to a very small extent or with the same intensity for all the plants in the same pit. In the literature, several authors have commented that the indirect selection of superior lines in segregating generations can be efficient as long as the plants are conducted in the field and under reduced spacing, as reported by Sampson (1971) in oats, McNeal et al. (1978) in wheat, Valentine (1983) in barley and Gravois & McNew (1993) in rice.

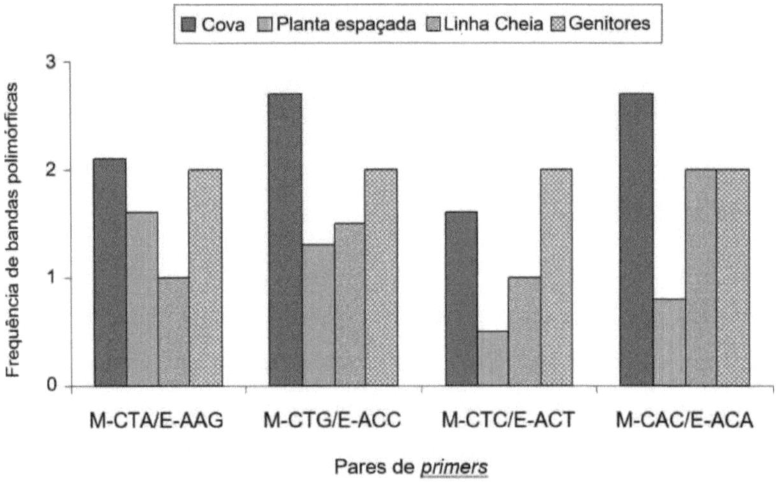

Figure 1 - Frequency of polymorphic bands for each pair of *primers*, in the comparison of *bulks* from the selection of heavier panicles with the less heavy panicles, in the three sowing methods and between the genitors, using the AFLP technique.

Figure 1 also shows that the frequency of polymorphic bands between the genitors UFRGS 14 (high panicle weight) and OR 2 (low panicle weight) was two polymorphic bands for each pair of *primers* tested. This fact allows us to form the hypothesis that there is genetic dissimilarity between the genitors used to obtain the population under study, dissimilarity which may be associated with panicle weight.

Based on the dissimilarity matrix obtained using Jaccard's similarity coefficient (Dias, 1998), the dendogram shown in Figure 2 was developed using the nearest neighbor technique. It can be seen that, in general, the treatments resulting from selection for high panicle weight, in the three sowing methods of the segregating population under study, were positioned close to each other, occupying the upper part of the dendogram, along with the UFRGS 14 sibling, which has a high panicle weight. On the other hand, the treatments derived from selection for low panicle weight, in the three sowing methods, occupied the lower part of the graph, together with the OR 2 genitor with low panicle weight.

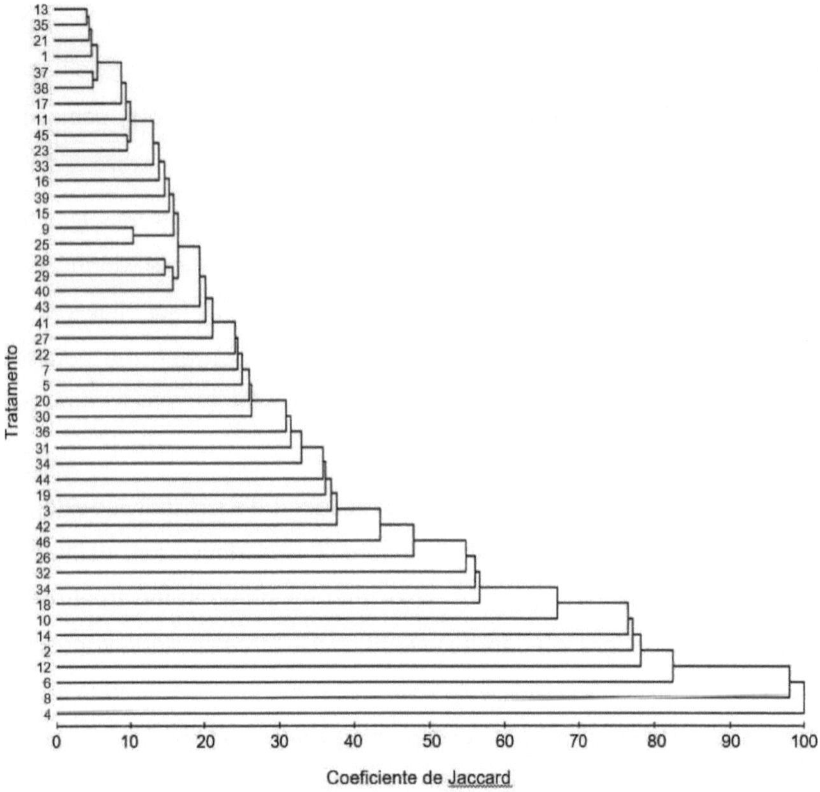

Figure 2 - Dendrogram representing the genetic dissimilarity between the treatments, obtained by the nearest neighbor technique, using the dissimilarity matrix obtained through the Jaccard coefficient,

These results allow us to formulate the hypothesis that the polymorphism found in this study, when comparing *bulks* from high-weight panicle selection against *bulks* from low-weight panicle selection, is likely to be associated with regions of the genome responsible for expressing the panicle weight trait in oats. Although a series of studies are needed to map these regions, the possibility of applying assisted selection for the panicle weight trait in oat breeding programs is extremely important, due to the high correlation between this trait and grain yield.

This initial study showed that the degree of polymorphism found between *bulks* selected for high and low panicle weight reveals candidate markers and allows us to test their association with regions of the genome responsible for expressing the panicle weight trait in oats.

3.3. Second stage of the study: material and methods

In 2003, a new, more in-depth study was carried out, using only the treatments from the selection in spaced plant, full line and the genitors, as shown in Table 4, totaling 28 treatments (26 bulks plus the genitors).

Sowing in DNA extraction cups, DNA extraction, application of the AFLP technique and analysis were similar to those mentioned above, only the dissimilarity study was not applied. The AFLP markers selected for this second study are shown in Table 5.

The bands were analyzed based on the electrophoretic pattern of the parents. In this way, all the polymorphic bands between the parents were evaluated in the segregating *bulks*.

Table 4 - Ratio of *bulks* formed with selection for panicle weight in the UFRGS 14 x OR 2 population in the two sowing methods plus the genitors.

Immediately	**Immediately**
1 Sel. spaced plant - top	14 Sel. spaced plant - bottom
2 Sel. spaced plant - bottom	15 Sel. spaced plant - top
3 Sel. spaced plant - top	16 Sel. spaced plant - bottom
4 Sel. spaced plant - bottom	17 Spaced plant seal - top
5 Sel. spaced plant - top	18 Sel. spaced plant - bottom
6 Sel. spaced plant - bottom	19 Spaced plant seal - top
7 Sel. spaced plant - top	20 Sel. spaced plant - bottom
8 Sel. spaced plant - bottom	21 Full line seal - top
9 Sel. spaced plant - top	22 Full line seal - bottom

10 Sel. spaced plant - bottom	23 Full line seal - top
11 Spaced plant seal - top	24 Full line seal - bottom
12 Sel. spaced plant - bottom	25 Genitor - UFRGS 14
13 Spaced plant seal - top	26 Parent - OR 2

Table 5 - List of the 24 AFLP *primer* combinations used in the study.

Cutting of the MseI restriction enzyme		Cutting the restriction enzyme EcoRI	
Primer	Selective bases	*Primer*	Selective bases
M	CTT	E	AGG
M	CTC	E	ACG
M	CTC	E	ACT
M	CTC	E	AGC
M	CTT	E	ACA
M	CTT	E	ACT
M	CAG	E	ACC
M	CAG	E	AGG
M	CAC	E	ACT
M	CAC	E	AGG
M	CAC	E	ACC
M	CAC	E	ACA
M	CAC	E	ACG
M	CAG	E	ACT
M	CAG	E	AAG
M	CTC	E	ACA
M	CTG	E	ACG

M	CAT	E	AGG
M	CTA	E	AGG
M	CTG	E	AAC
M	CTG	E	ACT
M	CAA	E	ACG
M	CAA	E	ACA
M	CAA	E	AGG

3.4. Second stage of the study: results and discussion

From the AFLP analysis using the 24 *primer* combinations, a total of 218 polymorphic markers were obtained. The number of polymorphic bands ranged from a maximum of 18 for the M- CTT; E-ACA *primer* combination to a minimum of 4 for the M-CAC; E-ACC combination (Table 6).

Table 6 - List of the 24 AFLP *primer* combinations used in the study and number of polymorphic bands obtained.

Primer Combination	Number of polymorphic bands	Primer Combination	Number of polymorphic bands
M - CTT; E - AGG	5	M - CAC; E - ACG	5
M - CTC; E - ACG	11	M - CAG; E - ACT	5
M - CTC; E - ACT	13	M - CAG; E - AAG	16
M - CTC; E - AGC	12	M - CTC; E - ACA	6
M - CTT; E - ACA	18	M - CTG; E - ACG	9
M - CTT; E - ACT	7	M - CAT; E - AGG	7
M - CAG; E - ACC	8	M - CTA; E - AGG	5
M - CAG; E - AGG	17	M - CTG; E - AAC	6

M - CAC; E - ACT	9	M - CTG; E - ACT	11
M - CAC; E - AGG	11	M - CAA; E - ACG	7
M - CAC; E - ACC	4	M - CAA; E - ACA	6
M - CAC; E - ACA	13	M - CAA; E - AGG	7

Band analysis did not reveal any marker fully associated with panicle weight in oats, possibly because this is a quantitative trait and several genes are involved in the expression of the phenotypic trait. However, it was possible to identify seven partially associated markers (Table 7).

Table 7 - List of the seven AFLP molecular markers partially associated with panicle weight in oats, *primer* combinations and percentage of association with the trait.

Marker	*Primer* combination	% association with low panicle weight	% association with high panicle weight
Lgf-044	M-CTT; E-ACA	8/13 (61,52%)	4/13 (30,77%)
Lgf-059	M-CTT; E-ACT	7/13 (53,85%)	2/13 (15,38%)
Lgf-083	M-CAG; E-AGG	2/13 (15,38%)	9/13 (69,23%)
Lgf-085	M-CAG; E-AGG	3/13 (23,08%)	6/13 (46,15%)
Lgf-102	M-CAC; E-ACC	8/13 (61,52%)	1/13 (7,69%)
Lgf-114	M-CAC; E-ACA	9/13 (69,23%)	4/13 (30,77%)
Lgf-126	M-CAG; E-ACT	0/13 (0%)	6/13 (46,15%)

Of the seven partially associated markers, *Lgf-083* (Figure 3); Lgf-102 (Figure 4) and *Lgf-126* (Figure 5) showed the highest percentages of association with the trait. The *Lgf-126* marker, although it did not show a considerable percentage of association with high panicle weight, showed 0% association with low panicle weight. Therefore, the potential use of this marker in future molecular marker-assisted selection studies is very important, as long as its association is proven in genetic constituencies with high panicle weight.

The subsequent elution and sequencing of these markers partially associated with panicle weight will allow them to be converted into potential co-dominant sequence-specific markers (SCAR - *Sequence Characterized Amplified Region*) (Hernandez et al., 1999) for use in molecular marker-assisted selection studies in oats.

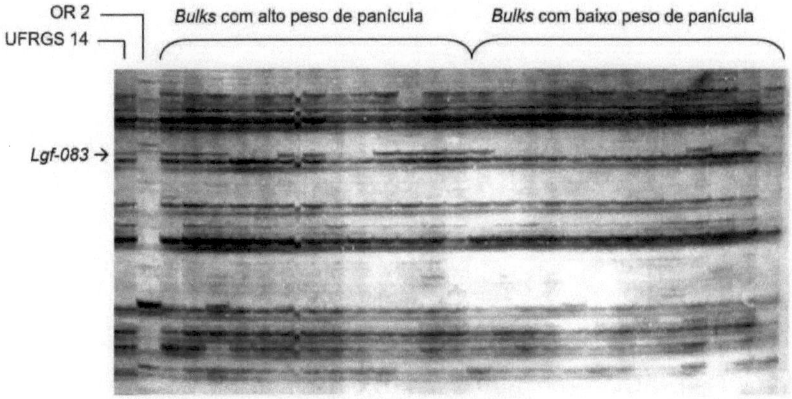

Figure 3 - Partial electrophoretic pattern obtained with the combination of *primers* M-CAG; E-AGG. The arrow indicates the AFLP marker *Lgf-083,* partially associated with panicle weight in oats.

Although none of the AFLP molecular markers showed a 100% association with the panicle weight trait, the results obtained are to be expected given the quantitative nature of the trait. The fact that several genes are involved in phenotypic expression makes it relatively difficult to find a situation where all the genes responsible for the trait are part of the genetic makeup of a single individual or family. This is why molecular marker-assisted selection, when it comes to quantitative traits, should be carried out using a combination of several molecular markers that are partially associated with the trait. The number of these markers and their percentage of association (duly proven) will be reflected in the efficiency of the selection.

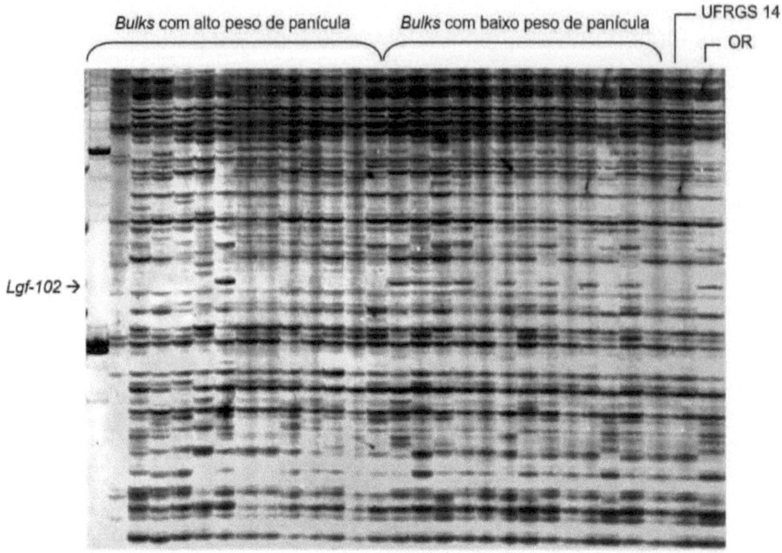

Figure 4 - Partial electrophoretic pattern obtained with the combination of *primers* M-CAC; E-ACC. The arrow indicates the AFLP marker *Lgf-102,* partially associated with panicle weight in oats.

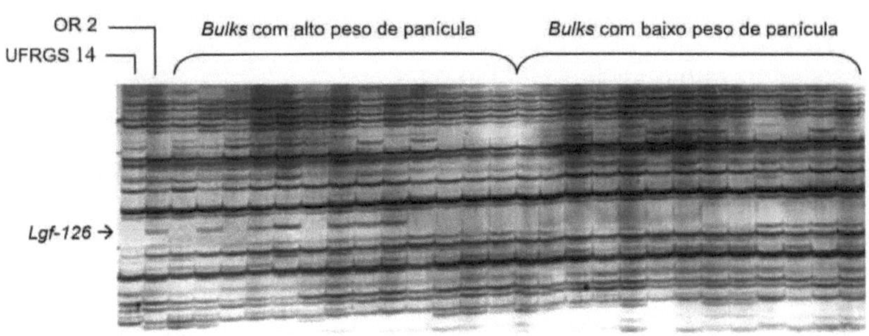

Figure 5 - Partial electrophoretic pattern obtained with the combination of *primers* M-CAG; E-ACT. The arrow indicates the AFLP marker *Lgf-126,* partially associated with panicle weight in oats.

Proving the association of these markers is of fundamental importance because the molecular marker techniques generally used to associate markers with phenotypic characteristics, although they act on the entire genome, only amplify a representative sample of the genome that is finally visualized. This amplified sample of the genome may not be the same in two successive amplification reactions.

Another drawback associated with the study of quantitative traits, apart from the number of genes involved, is the genotype-environment interaction. Each QTL involved has an interaction with the environment that is independent of the other QTLs, and this interaction varies according to location and time of year. This can lead to unstable associations between markers and QTLs in different environments, or to the extrapolation of markers from one population to another. Markers associated with a QTL in one population will not necessarily be associated with the same QTL in another, making these markers undesirable for selection (Schnider et al. 1997).

For the association of molecular markers involved with quantitative traits, it is recommended that this is done when the segregating populations have been conducted in competitive environments, with reduced spacing between plants (high competitiveness), so that the participation of the genotype in the expression of the trait is maximized (Geadelmann & Frey 1975). The greater the participation of the genotype in character expression, the greater the efficiency and reliability of molecular markers.

In this second stage of the study, it was observed that the molecular marker technique proved to be efficient in revealing the polymorphism existing in segregating oat populations, even in populations with high homozygosity. Analysis by segregating *bulks* maximizes the identification of genomic regions associated with traits of interest when analysed with molecular markers, provided that the effect of the environment is properly circumvented and phenotypic selection is well conducted.

3.5. Third stage of the study: material and methods

Another study was carried out in 2003, with some treatments remaining, as shown in Table 8, making a total of 25 treatments (23 *bulks* plus the genitors).

Table 8 - Ratio of *bulks* formed with selection for panicle weight in the UFRGS 14 x OR 2 population in the two sowing methods plus the genitors.

	Treatment	T reatment
1	Sel. cova - top	13 Spaced plant seal - top
2	Pit seal - bottom	14 Sel. spaced plant - bottom
3	Sel. cova - top	15 Sel. spaced plant - top
4	Pit seal - bottom	16 Sel. spaced plant - top
5	Sel. cova - top	17 Sel. spaced plant - bottom
6	Pit seal - bottom	18 Sel. spaced plant - top
7	Sel. cova - top	19 Sel. spaced plant - bottom
8	Pit seal - bottom	20 Sel. spaced plant - top
9	Sel. cova - top	21Sel . spaced plant - bottom
10	Pit seal - bottom	22 Spaced plant seal - top
11	Sel. cova - top	23 Sel. spaced plant - bottom
12	Pit seal - bottom	24 Genitor - UFRGS 14
		25 Parent - OR 2

Sowing in DNA extraction cups, DNA extraction, application of the AFLP technique and analysis were similar to those mentioned above. The AFLP markers selected for this study were the same as those used in the previous work, mentioned in Table 5. All the polymorphic markers between the genitors of the segregating population were evaluated for presence (1) and absence (0) in the 23 segregating blocks.

The data was used to construct a binary matrix for analysis. Analyses of genetic similarity, co-phenetic matrix, matrix comparison and cluster analysis were carried out using the computer program NTSyS pc 2.1 (Rohlf, 2000). Genetic similarity was estimated using the Nei and Li (1979) coefficient. The variances and means were estimated for the two similarity matrices and the means were compared using the t-test (Beinguelman, 2002). The average genetic similarity was used as the cut-off point for forming the groups. The 23 blocks were grouped based on the genetic similarity matrix using the UPGMA method (*Unweighted Pair-Group Method with arithmetic Averages*).

3.6. Second stage of the study: results and discussion

From the AFLP analysis using the 24 *primer* combinations, a total of 218 polymorphic markers were obtained. The number of polymorphic markers ranged from a maximum of 18 for the *Mse* I- CTT; *Eco* RI-ACA primer combination to a minimum of 4 for the *Mse* I-CAC; *Eco* RI- ACC combination.

Pit sowing method: The genetic similarity between the segregating blocks, when conducted using the pit sowing method, was between 0.51 and 0.76. The value of the co-phenetic matrix (r) (Rohlf & Sokal, 1981), obtained from comparing the similarity matrices and the dendogram, was 0.86. This value, considered highly representative, reflects the accuracy of the dendogram in graphically representing the similarity data between the genotypes. However, based on the average genetic similarity for forming the clusters, it was not possible to establish significant associations between the segregating blocks and the panicle weight trait. The most similar possible groups of genotypes were formed by high and low panicle weight segregating blocks (Figure 6).

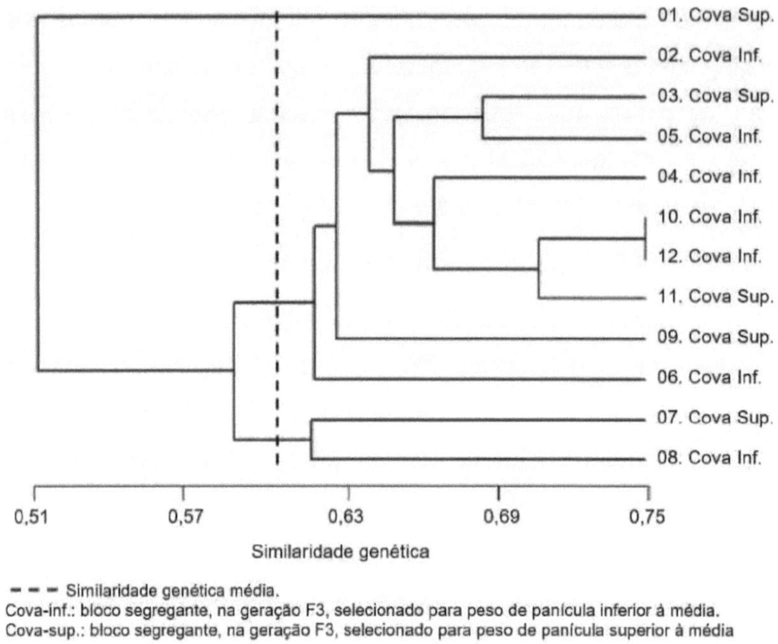

Figure 6 - Dendogram obtained from AFLP molecular markers using the UPGMA clustering method, for data from plants grown using the pit method in a segregating oat population for panicle weight.

For the spaced plant sowing method, the genetic similarity between the segregating blocks, when conducted using the spaced plant sowing method, was between 0.62 and 0.83. The value of the cofenetic matrix (r) (Rohlf and Sokal, 1981), obtained from comparing the similarity matrices and the dendogram, although lower than that obtained with the pit sowing method, was 0.77. This value, considered representative, reflects the accuracy of the dendogram in graphically representing the similarity data between the genotypes. As was the case with the pit method, the genetic similarity calculated between the segregating blocks using the spaced plant method did not allow a good association to be made between the panicle weight trait and the segregating blocks.

The average genetic similarity was used as the cut-off point for forming the groups (Figure 7). The analysis of the comparison of means using the t-test between the two similarity matrices, for both sowing methods, showed a value of 0.75, indicating that they do not differ significantly at a 1% significance level. This may be due to the fact that the segregating blocks, conducted using the two methods, are derived from the same cross.

The data from the cluster analysis based on molecular data do not agree with the postulates of Sampson (1971), in which panicle weight in oats has great potential for the indirect selection of superior lines in segregating generations, as long as the selection is carried out in the field and on plants with reduced spacing (high competitiveness). According to Geadelmann & Frey (1975), the effect of direct or indirect selection for grain yield found in a competitive environment, where natural selection occurs, promotes a greater selection gain compared to non-competitive environments (spaced plants). However, the results obtained in this work showed that the genetic base of the segregating population remained narrower when conducted using the spaced plant method in a non-competitive environment (between 0.62 and 0.83), compared to the genetic base of the segregating population conducted using the pit method (between 0.51 and 0.76). In addition, the average genetic similarity values in the pit method (0.60) were lower than in the spaced plant method (0.67), showing that, even under conditions of low competitiveness, the segregating blocks remained more genetically similar than under conditions of high competitiveness between plants.

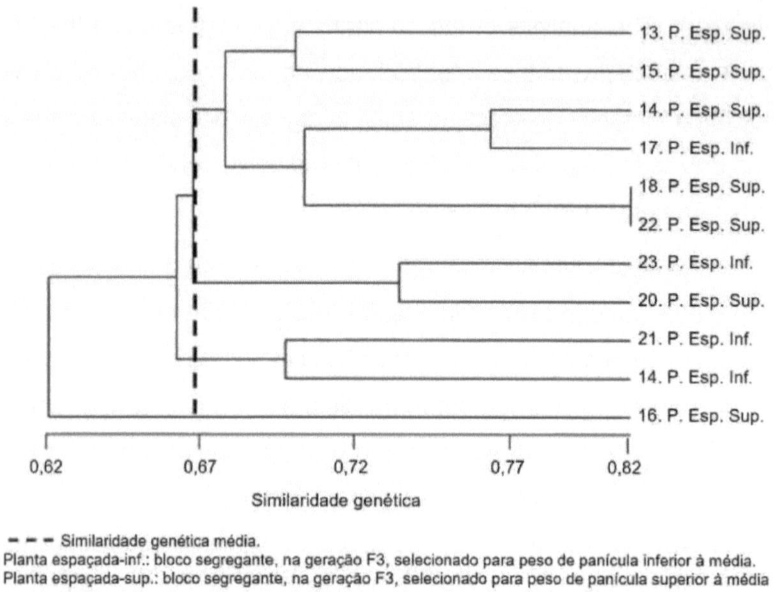

Figure 7 - Dendogram obtained based on AFLP molecular markers using the UPGMA clustering method, for data from plants conducted by the spaced plant method from a segregating oat population for panicle weight.

However, grouping analyses of segregating blocks based on molecular genetic similarity revealed that there is no significant variation in the genetic pool of the populations in the F3 generation, when conducted using the pit and spaced plant methods. It is likely that the selection carried out on the populations was not enough to cause significant segregation of genes which would allow the blocks to be separated using the two sowing methods. In addition, the panicle weight trait is significantly affected by the environment in phenotypic expression, which makes it difficult to identify genetic constituencies or segregating blocks using molecular markers in early generations.

We found that there was genetic dissimilarity between the segregating blocks conducted using the pit sowing and spaced plant methods. The selection pressure exerted was not enough to cause segregation that would lead to the accumulation of distinct genes for each sowing method.

4. BIBLIOGRAPHICAL REFERENCES

AJMONE MARSAN P, CASTIGLIONI P, FUSARI F, KUIPER M, MOTTO M. (1998) Genetic diversity and its relationship to hybrid performance in maize as revealed by RFLP and AFLP markers. **Theor. Appl. Genet.** 96: 219-227.

ALLARD RW (1999) **Principles of plant breeding.** New York: J. Wiley. 485 p.

ALLEN FL, COMSTOCK RE, RASMUSSON DC (1977) Optimal environments for yield testing. **Crop Science** 17: 747-751.

ATLIN GN, FREY KJ (1990) Selection oat lines for yield in low-productivity environments. **Crop Science** 30: 556-561.

BALLVORA A, HESSELBACH J, NIEWOHNER J, LEISTER D, SALAMINI F, GEBHARDT C (1995) Marker enrichment and high-resolution map of the segment of potato chromosome VII harbouring the nematode resistance gene *Gro1*. **Mol. Gen. Genet**. 249: 82-90.

BARRETT BA, KIDWELL KK, FOX PN (1998) Comparison of AFLP and pedigree-based genetic diversity assessment methods using wheat cultivars from the Pacific Northwest. **Crop Science** 38: 1271-1278.

BARRETT BA, KIDWELL KK. (1998) AFLP-based genetic diversity assessment among wheat cultivars from the Pacific Northwest. **Crop Science** 38: 1261-1271.

BECKER J, VOS P, KUIPER M, SALAMINI F, HEUN M. (1995) Combined mapping of AFLP and RFLP markers in barley. **Mol. Gen. Genet**. 249: 65-73.

BEINGUELMAN B (2002) **Curso pràtico de bioestatistica.** 5. ed. Ribeirao Preto: Fundaçâo de pesquisas Cientificas de Ribeirao Preto. 274p.

BLUM A (1998) **Plant breeding for stress environments**. Florida: CRC Press.

BORNET B, BRANCHARD M (2001) Nonanchored Inter Simple Sequence Repeat (ISSR) Markers: Reproducible and Specific Tools for Genome Fingerprinting. **Plant Molecular Biology Reporter** 19: 209-215.

BOTSTEIN DR, WHITE RL, SKOLNICK M, DAVIS RW (1980) Construction of a genetic linkage map in man using restriction fragment length polymorphisms. **Am. J. Jum. Genet.** 32: 314-331.

BRIARD M, CLERA VLE, GNZEBELUS D, SENALIK D, SIMON PW (2000) Modified Protocols for rapid carrot genomic DNA extraction and AFLP™ analysis using silver stain on radioisotopes. **Plant Molecular Biology Reporter** 18: 235-241.

BROWN CM, FORSBERG RA (1987) Oat. In: FEHR, W.R. **Principles of cultivar development.** New York: Crop Species. 760p.

BURKHAMER RL, LANNING SP, MARTENS RJ, MARTIN JM, TALBERT LE. (1998) Predicting progeny variance from parental divergence in hard red spring wheat. **Crop Science** 38: 243-248.

BYRNE PF, BOLANOS J, EDMEADES GO, EATON DL (1995) Gain from selection under drought versus multilocation testing in related tropical maize populations. **Crop Science** 35: 63-69, 1995.

CALHOUN DS, GEBEYEHU G, MIRANDA A, RAJARAM S, VAN GINKEL M (1994) Choosing evaluation environments to increase wheat grain yield under drought conditions. **Crop Science** 34: 673-678.

CARVALHO FIF (1982) Quantitative genetics. In: OSÓRIO EA. **Wheat in Brazil.** Sâo Paulo: Fundaçâo Cargil. chap.3, p.63-94.

CARVALHO FIF, FEDERIZZI LC (1989) **Evoluçâo da cultura de aveia no sul do Brasil.** Porto Alegre: Trigo e Soja. v.102, p.16-19.

CASLER MD (1995) Patterns of variation in a collection of perennial ryegrass accessions. **Crop Science** 35: 1169-1177.

CECCARELLI S (1989) Wide adaptation: How wide? **Euphytica** 40:197-205.

CECCARELLI S, GRANDO S, IMPIGLIA A (1998) Choice of selection strategy in breeding barley for stress environments. **Euphytica** 103: 307-318.

CHANDHANAMUTTA P, FREY KJ (1973) Indirect mass selection for grain yield in oat populations. **Crop Science** 13: 470-473.

CHAPKO LB, BRINKMAN MA Interrelationships between panicle weight, grain yield on grain yield components in oat. **Crop Science** 31: 878-882.

COFFMAN FA (1961) **Oats and oat improvement.** Medison: the American Society of Agronomy. 650p.

CRUZ CD (1990) **Aplicaçâo de algumas técnicas multivariadas no melhoramento de plantas.** Piracicaba: ESALQ. Doctoral thesis 188p.

CRUZ CD (2001) **Programa Genes: Aplicativo computacional em genètica e estatistica.** Viçosa: Editora UFV. 648p.

CRUZ CD, CASTOLDI FL (1991) Decomposition of the genotype x environment interaction into simple and complex parts. **Revista Ceres** 38: 422-430.

CRUZ CD, REGAZZI AJ (1997) **Biometric models applied to genetic improvement.** 2ed. Viçosa: Editora UFV. 390p.

CRUZ PJ, CARVALHO FIF, FEDERIZZI LC (1983) Population effects and selection methods applied in segregating wheat generations. **Pesquisa Agropecuària Brasileira** 18: 533-541.

DOYLE JJ, DOYLE JL (1987) Isolation of plant DNA from fhesh tissue. **Focus** 12: 13-15.

ELLIS RP, MCNICOL JW, BAIRD E, BOOTH A, LAWRENCE P, THOMAS B, POWELL W. (1997) The use of AFLPs to examine genetic relatedness in barley. **Mol. Breed.** 3: 359-369.

FALCONER DS (1981) **Introduction to quantitative genetics.** Viçosa: Editora UFV. 279p.

FASOULAS A (1973) A **new approach to breeding superior yielding varieties**. Greece: Aristotelian University of Thessaloniki. 41p. (Publication 3).

FEDERIZZI LC, MILACH SCK, PACHECO MT, NETO JFB, SERENO MJCM (1999) **Oat Improvement.** In: BORÉM A. Improvement of Cultivated Species. Viçosa: Editora UFV. p.131-157.

FEDERIZZI LC, QUALSET CO (1989) Genetics of plant height reduction and panicle type in oat. **Crop Science** 29: 551-557.

GAEDELMANN JL, FREY KJ (1975) Direct and indirect mass selection for grain yield in bulk oat populations. **Crop Science** 15: 190-194.

GAUR PC, GRUPTA PK, KISHORI H (1978) Studies on genetic divergence in potato. **Euphytica** 27: 316-368.

GRAVOIS KA, MCNEW RW (1993) Genetic relationships among and selection for rice yield and yield components. **Crop Science** 33: 249-252.

HERNANDEZ P, MARTiN A, DORADO G (1999) Development of SCARs by direct sequencing of RAPD products: a practical tool for the introgression and marker-assisted selection of wheat. **Molecular Breeding** 5: 245-253.

HILL M, WITSENBOER H, ZABEAU M, VOS P, KESSELI R, MICHELMORE R (1996) PCR-based "fingerprinting using AFLPs as a tool for studying genetic relationships in *Lactuca* spp". **Theor. Appl. Genet.** 93: 1202-1210.

HONGTRAKUL V, HUESTIS GM, KNAPP SJ (1997) Amplified fragment length polymorphisms as a tool for DNA fingerprinting sun-flower germplasm: genetic diversity among oilseed inbred lines. **Theor. Appl. Genet.** 95: 400407.

KEIM P, SCHUPP JM, TRAVIS SE, CLAYTON K, ZHU T, SHI LIANG, FERREIRA A, WEBB DM. (1997) A high-density soybean genetic map based on AFLP markers. **Crop Science** 37: 537-543.

KNOTT DR (1972) Effects of selection for F2 plant yield on subsequent generations in wheat. **Canadian Journal Plant Science** 52: 721-726.

MACHADO CF (1999) **Procedures for choosing bean genitors**. Lavras: UFLA. Master's dissertation. 118p.

MAHESWARAN M, SUBUDHI PK, NANDI S, XU JC, PARCO A, YANG DC, HUANG N (1997) Polymorphism, distribution, and segregation of AFLP markers in a doubled-haploid rice population. **Theor. Appl. Genet.** 94: 39-45.

McGINNIS RG, SHEBESKI LH (1968) **The realibility of single plant selection for yield in F2.** In: international Wheat Genetics Symposium. Procceding, Canberra: Australian Academy of Science. p.410-415.

McNEAL FH, QUALSET CO, BALDRIGE DE, STEWART ER (1978) Selection for yield and yield components in wheat. **Crop Science** 18: 795799.

MEKSEM K, LEISTER D, PELEMAN J, ZABEAU M, SALAMINI F, GEBHARDT C (1995) A high-resolution map of the vicinity of the R1 Locus on chromosome V of potato based on RFLP and AFLP markers. **Mol. Gen. Genet.** 249: 74-81.

MICHELMORE RW, PARAN I, KESSELI RV (1991) Identification of markers to disease-resistance genes by bulked segregant analyses: a rapid method detect markers in specific genomic regions by using segregating populations. **Proc. Natl. Acad. Sci.** 88: 9828-9832.

MORGANTE M, OLIVIERI AM (1993) PCR-amplified microsatellites as markers in plant genetics. **The Plant Journal** 3: 175-182.

NEI M, LI WH (1979) Mathematical model for studying genetic variation in terms of restriction endonucleases. **Proceedings National Academic Sciences** 76: 5269-5273.

PAKNIYAT H, POWELL W, BAIRD E, HANDLEY LL, ROBINSON D, SCRIMGEOUR CM, NEVO E, HACKETT CA, CALIGARI PDS, FORSTER BP (1997) AFLP variation in wild barley (*Hordeum spontaneum* C. Koch) with reference to salt tolerance and associated ecogeography. **Genome** 40: 332341.

POWELL W, THOMAS WTB, BAIRD E, LAWRENCE P, BOOTH A, HARROWER B, MCNICOL JW, WAUGH R (1997) Analysis of quantitative traits in barley by the use of amplified fragment length polymorphisms. **Heredity** 79: 48-59.

QI X, LINDHOUT P (1997) Development of AFLP markers in barley. **Mol. Gen. Genet**. 254: 330-336.

QUAIL KJ, WOOD JT (1989) Early generation selection in wheat. I. Yield potential. **Australian Jounal Agriculture Research** 40: 1117-1133.

ROA AC, MAYA MM, DUQUE MC, TOHME J, ALLEM AC, BONIERBALE MW (1997) AFLP analysis of relationships among cassava and other *Manihot* species. **Theor. Appl. Genet.** 95: 741-750.

ROHLF FJ, SOKAL RR (1981) Comparing numerical taxonomic studies. **Systematic zoology** 30: 459-490.

ROLHF FJ (2000) **NTSYS-pc: Numerical taxonomy and multivariate analysis system.** Version 2.1. New York: Exeter Publications. 38p.

SAMPSON DR (1971) Additive and non additive genetic variances and genotype correlations for yield and other traits in oats. **Canadian Journal Genetics Cytology** 13: 864-872.

SANTOS CAF, REIS MS, SEDIYAMA CS, CRUZ CD, SEDIYAMA T (1995) Genetic parameters and indirect selection in F6 progenies of a soybean (*Glycine Max* (L.) Merrill) cross. **Revista Ceres** 42: 155-166.

SCHNEIDER KA, BROTHERS ME, KELLY JD (1997) Marker Assisted Selection to Improve Drought Resistance in Common Bean. **Crop Science** 37:51-60.

SCHUT JW, QI X, STAM P (1997) Association between relationship measures based on AFLP markers, pedigree data and morphological traits in barley. **Theor. Appl. Genet.** 95: 1161-1168.

SEITZER JF, EVANS LE (1978) Yield gains in wheat by the pedigree method of selection and two early tests. **Zeiitschrift für Pflanzenzüchtung** 80: 1-10.

SINGH D (1981) The relative importance of characters affecting genetic divergence. **The Indian Journal of Genetics and Plant Breeding** 41: 237245.

TAVARES MJCMS, ZANETTINI MHB, CARVALHO FIF (1993) Origin and evolution of the *Avena* genus: its implications for genetic improvement.

Pesquisa Agropecuâria Brasileira 28: 499-507.

VALENTINE J (1983) **Early generation selection for yield in cereals.** In: LANGE W. Efficiency in plant breeding. European Congress of Resources Plant Breeding, 10. Eucarpia: Wageningen. p.19-24.

VANTOAI TT, PENG J, St MARTIN SK (1997) Using AFLP markers to determine the genomic contribution of parents to populations. **Crop Science** 37: 1370-1373.

VOS P, HOGRES R, BLEEKER M, REIJANS M, LEE T, HORNES M, FRITJERS A, POT J, PELEMAN J, KUIPER M, ZABEU M (1995) AFLP: a new technique for DNA fingerprinting. **Nucl. Ac. Res**., 23: 4407-4414.

WANG YH, THOMAS CE, DEAN RA (1997) A genetic map of melon (*Cucumis melo* L.) based on amplified fragment length polymorphism (AFLP) markers. **Theor. Appl. Genet.** 95: 791-798.

WILLIAMS JGK, KUBELIK AR, LIVAK KJ, RAFALSKY JA, TINGEY SV (1990) DNA polymorphisms amplified by arbitrary primers are useful as genetic markers. **Nucleic Acids Research** 18: 6531-653.

MIX
Papier aus verantwortungsvollen Quellen
Paper from responsible sources
FSC® C105338

FSC
www.fsc.org

Printed by Books on Demand GmbH, Norderstedt / Germany